Stuck in a Wet Suit

By Carmel Reilly

Dad, Papa and Carly were going away on a boat.

Carly got out her suit case.

"I can not wait to go on the boat!" said Papa.

"Pack your swim suit, Carly," said Dad.
"We will swim in the sea."

"Pack your wet suit, too,"
said Papa.
"The sea might be cold."

Papa and Dad got meat,
fruit and other things
to take on the boat.

Papa drove them
to the dock.

Then, they wheeled their
suit cases onto the boat.

Dad sailed the boat away
from the dock.

Papa and Carly sat on the deck
with a plate of fruit.

They had sailed far out to sea.

"Let's swim!" said Carly.
"I will put on my swim suit!"

"Let's put on our wet suits,"
said Dad.
"That sea looks chilly!"

"I will take photos," said Papa.

Carly and Dad spotted
some fish in the sea!

Then Carly got cold.

She was glad of her wet suit.

Dad tugged his wet suit zip.
But it was **stuck**!

Carly tugged, and Papa tugged,
but it was no good.

"I can not keep my wet suit on the whole trip!" said Dad.

"We will have to rip the zip!" said Papa.

"It's not funny!" said Dad.

Papa cut some fruit
for Dad and Carly.

"I hope the sea heats up!"
said Dad.

CHECKING FOR MEANING

1. Where were Dad, Papa and Carly going? *(Literal)*

2. What did Papa and Dad take on the boat to eat? *(Literal)*

3. Why did Dad want the sea to heat up? *(Inferential)*

EXTENDING VOCABULARY

suit	What is a *suit*? Which suits are mentioned in the story? E.g. wet suit, swim suit. Is a suit one or two pieces of clothing, or can it be either?
to/too	Discuss the difference between the words *to* and *too*. Explain that *to* means *towards*, and *too* means *also, as well as,* or *extremely*.
fruit	What is *fruit*? What are the names of some fruits you like to eat? E.g. apples, bananas, pineapples, pears, grapes.

MOVING BEYOND THE TEXT

1. Talk about the people who wear a wet suit and why they need one.

2. Where are safe places to swim in the sea?

3. Discuss why the water in the sea is colder than the water in a swimming pool.

4. What equipment is needed to be able to see under the water? Can you swim under the water to see the fish and plants? What else do you need?

SPEED SOUNDS

oo	ue	ew	ui	u_e

ou	u	oe	o

PRACTICE WORDS

to

suit

fruit

too

suits